Luther and the Reformation

Luther and the Reformation

How a Monk Discovered the Gospel

R.C. SPROUL

 LIGONIER MINISTRIES

Luther and the Reformation: How a Monk Discovered the Gospel
© 2021 by the R.C. Sproul Trust

Ligonier Ministries
421 Ligonier Court, Sanford, FL 32771
Ligonier.org

Printed in Ann Arbor, Michigan
Cushing-Malloy, Inc.
0001021
First edition

ISBN 978-1-64289-373-1 (Paperback)
ISBN 978-1-64289-374-8 (ePub)
ISBN 978-1-64289-375-5 (Kindle)

Cover design: Ligonier Creative
Interior typeset: Katherine Lloyd, The DESK

Scripture quotations are from the ESV® Bible (The Holy Bible,
English Standard Version®), copyright © 2001 by Crossway, a
publishing ministry of Good News Publishers. Used by permission. All rights reserved.

Library of Congress Control Number: 2021936971

Contents

From Luther to the Lightning Bolt

Above the modern city of Geneva, Switzerland, stands a section called the Old Town. In the center of the Old Town is a large walking park that features a giant wall of marble called the Reformation Wall. The Reformation Wall features the likenesses of Martin Luther, Philip Melanchthon, John Calvin, Theodore Beza, John Knox, Martin Bucer, Huldrych Zwingli, and a few others. And chiseled into the stone at the top of the wall are the words *Post tenebras lux*— "After darkness, light." This became the motto of the sixteenth-century Reformation.

What was this darkness, this *tenebras*? From the Reformation standpoint, the darkness refers to what had happened to the Roman Catholic Church during the Middle Ages. The church had been experiencing a steady change in its understanding of biblical Christianity, most importantly in its understanding of salvation. What had developed in Rome at this time is what we call *sacerdotalism*—the idea that salvation is accomplished chiefly through the ministrations of the church, through the priesthood, and particularly through the administration of the sacraments. This system of salvation that developed within the Roman Catholic Church came to a crisis with the sixteenth-century Reformation.

But before we examine the historical incidents that provoked this crisis and the people whom God used to bring it to pass, I want to make an important distinction: the Reformers themselves considered their work to be that of reformation, not revolution. They did not see their activities as an organized revolt against the church or against historic Christianity. In many ways, like the eighth- and seventh-century BC prophets of Israel, the Reformers saw their task as calling God's people back to their founding. They wanted the church to return to its original forms and to the original theology of the Apostolic church. That is, the Reformers were not trying to create something new.

In 1504, Martin Luther was twenty-one years old. He had completed his master of arts and had enrolled in law school. By age twenty-one, Luther had already distinguished himself with his intelligence. He had been raised in the classical educational system, under which students were required to speak fluent Latin, the language of the university. It was the language of those involved in jurisprudence. It was the language of theologians and of physicians and other professionals. And so Luther's training to become a lawyer served him quite well throughout his lifetime.

To get a sense of where Luther's life fit in Western history, imagine this. He was born in 1483. That means that he was nine years old when Christopher Columbus landed in the New World. The Western world at this time was experiencing all kinds of tumultuous changes.

Luther's father and mother had been peasants in

Germany near the Thuringian Forest. Hans Luther left the fields of the farm and became a miner. He was so successful in the mining industry of the region that through his managerial and entrepreneurial skills he managed to become an owner of six foundries and elevated the economic station of his family significantly. But his great dream was the education of his son Martin. He would have a son who would be a prominent lawyer, who would become wealthy, and who would be able to care for his parents in their old age. Everything was progressing nicely in this direction in Luther's early years of education. Martin had a reputation for remarkable brilliance in the field of law. Later, his role in the Protestant Reformation greatly benefited from his understanding of law, because he took the skills and the education that he had in jurisprudence and applied it to his study of biblical law.

The crisis that would change Luther's life, and that would change the world forever, took place in July 1505, when Luther was walking home from the university. In the middle of the day, a sudden thunderstorm of great ferocity arose. Suddenly a lightning bolt struck the ground just a few feet from where Luther was walking; it was so close to him that it knocked him on the ground. He saw this as a message from God. He was terrified, and he cried out in his fear, "Help me, St. Anne; I will become a monk."

He made his appeal to St. Anne, the mother of Mary, because she was the patron saint for miners, and she had a prominent place in the daily prayers within the Luther household. So in this moment of crisis, Luther called to heaven for the protection of St. Anne. And true to this vow, he moved to the Augustinian monastery in the city of Erfurt. He chose to enter that particular monastery because it was known as the most rigorous and demanding of the various monastic orders, reflecting the depth of its founder, Augustine of Hippo.

Luther presented himself at the front door of the monastery, was welcomed by the prior, and was asked the question that every novice was asked: "What do you seek?" Luther answered, "God's grace and your mercy." And so he was admitted into the order as a novice. At the end of his ordination day, he stood as a monk—an occasion filled with more irony than seen in any other moment in church history. The custom for ordination into the priesthood or to the monastic orders was for each man to present himself at the front of the chancel's stairs. He had to prostrate himself on the floor with his arms extended, his body forming the shape of a cross, and he would be garbed in most uncomfortable clothes. In this state of humiliation, the process of ordination would proceed. So where is the irony?

To explain that, I must recall a tour of Luther's Germany I led years ago. We visited all the important cities of Luther's life. We went to the city of his birth, Eisleben, which in the providence of God also became the city of his death. We went to Wittenberg, where he taught at the university and where he posted the Ninety-Five Theses on the Castle Church door. We went to Worms, where the imperial diet was held in 1521. We went to Leipzig, where an important disputation took place. And of course, we visited Erfurt and the site where Luther had been ordained. The year of our tour was a celebration of Luther, and portraits of Luther were all over what was then East Germany. Every church building and many billboards featured a portrait of Martin Luther against the background of the silhouette of a swan. I asked why the image of the swan adorned these posters with the portrait of Martin Luther, and I learned that the imagery dated back to events that had taken place in Bohemia in the city of Prague. A noted professor in that area had published works declaring that the Scriptures alone contained the inspired Word of God and could not be equaled by the edicts and teachings of the church. For that and other doctrines he was teaching, he ran into problems with the established church and was put on trial as a heretic. The man's name was Jan Hus. *Hus* in the Czech language means "goose." When Hus would not recant his writings, the presiding bishop sentenced him to be burned at the stake. As Hus was about to be executed, he said to the presiding bishop, "You may burn this goose, but there will come after me a swan, whom you will not be able to silence," and that story became widely known throughout Europe. So when Luther appeared on the scene, he was welcomed as the prophetic fulfillment of Jan Hus' idea of the swan who would come.

Here's the irony. When Luther presented himself for ordination at the chancel steps at the Erfurt monastery and lay on the ground with his arms outstretched, he was right in front of the altar, and buried in front of the altar under the stones of the chapel was the bishop who had condemned Jan Hus to death. When Hus said to the bishop, "You may burn this goose, but there will come a swan whom you will not be able to silence," I'd like to think that the bishop said to Hus, "Over my dead body!"

In his early years, Luther tended to have a crisis about every five years. In 1505 came the lightning bolt. It was the lightning bolt that changed the world. He faced another crisis in 1510 when he made a visit to Rome and still a third crisis in 1515 when he understood the gospel for the first time in his life. But first we have to understand what happened to him when he entered the monastery.

Things were not good at home. Father Hans was furious with his son for disappointing him by not pursuing a career in law. When Luther entered the monastery, he vowed to become the best monk that he could possibly be. Later he would reflect and say, "If anyone was ever going to make it to heaven through monkery, it was I." And so he engaged in the rigorous schedule of the monastic life. Scheduled during the day were several times of prayer, which had an impact on the rest of his life. Luther was a disciplined man of prayer as long as he lived. But not only that, he participated in the practice of the daily confessional. Each monk had a father confessor with whom he had to meet every day as a matter of religious discipline. Luther gave nothing but vexation to his father confessor and the other authorities in the monastery. The other brothers would confess: "Father, I have sinned in the last twenty-four hours. I coveted Brother Jonathan's dinner last night, and I stayed up five minutes past lights-out." They would confess their sins in five minutes, get their absolution, and then go back to their tasks in the monastery. But Brother Luther would come and confess his sins of the last twenty-four hours for twenty minutes, half an hour, an hour, and sometimes two or three hours, until the confessor became exasperated with him. The confessor would say: "Brother Martin, don't come to me with these minor infractions. If you are going to sin, give me something worth forgiving."

But Luther's mind worked this way. He was a student of the law. He pored over the law meticulously. He realized, for example, that the Great Commandment was to love the Lord his God with all his might and all his soul and all his strength and to love his neighbor as much as he loved himself, and he knew that he hadn't obeyed this commandment for a single hour. As he applied the fullness of the depths of God's law to his own life, all he could see was guilt. He was driven by a passion to experience forgiveness that was real and lasting, but this passion was never fulfilled in the monastery.

2

Monastery
and Rome Crisis

How could one man in an obscure German town
stand alone against the whole Roman Catholic
Church? What drove Martin Luther with such passion? Scholars and professionals within the field of
psychology have wondered whether he was neurotic
or even psychotic.[*] When reading Luther's volumi-
nous writings, you can't help but notice his frequent
use of intemperate language. In Luther's day, polemical

---

[*] See R.C. Sproul, *The Holiness of God* (Wheaton, Ill.: Tyndale, 1985), particularly chapter 5, "The Insanity of Luther."

language and vitriolic attacks on one's enemy were commonplace, and Luther was a master of those forms of debate. He often called those who disagreed with him "dogs." When the church would react to something he wrote, Luther would say, "The dogs are starting to bark." And that kind of language was mild for Luther.

Psychologists have also focused on other aspects of Luther's life. He had a preoccupation with guilt during his days in the monastery. Nothing he did gave him peace of mind or quieted his conscience. He would spend long periods of time in the confessional. Often after spending hours confessing his sins to the father confessor and receiving the absolution, he'd go back to his cell and suddenly remember a sin that he had forgotten to confess. He was also involved in self-flagellation and the rigorous forms of asceticism that monks used to purge themselves of any evil thoughts. But Luther was in a class by himself in inflicting punishment on his own person to salve his conscience.

Now, we have to understand the level of corruption among the clergy in the medieval church. This was the age of the Medici and the Borgia popes, who were renowned for their scandalous ways. Yet people still believed that the best way to ensure one's personal salvation was to enter into holy orders, to have a holy vocation, and particularly to enter a monastery. That gave a person an inside road to sanctification and to reaching heaven's door. So Luther was determined that through the rigors of the monastic life, he would gain the peace of mind that he so desperately sought. On one occasion, he was asked, "Brother Martin, do you love God?" He said: "Love God? Love God? Sometimes I hate Him. I see Christ as a furious judge with the sword of judgment in His hand, coming after me."

Modern psychiatrists have said that this morbid sense of unsettled conscience is not rational. It's not sane. Think about that. People who are losing touch with reality are said to have lost the normal ability to cope with fears and guilt. For example, there's a story of a man who wouldn't leave his home. He wouldn't even go out on a picnic because he was so afraid of the dangers that were inherent in picnic sites. So his wife took him to a psychiatrist, who asked the man, "Why are you so afraid to go on a picnic?" He said: "If I go on a picnic, the food is outside in the sun. I could get food poisoning and die. Not only that, there could be snakes in the grass. A poisonous snake could bite me and kill me. Or if I drive to the picnic site, I might get hit by a car and be killed. The world out there is filled with danger every minute." What could the psychiatrist say? "There's no risk in riding in an automobile"? Of course there's risk in riding in an automobile. "There's no risk of getting food poisoning"? Of course there's a risk of getting food poisoning. "No risk of getting bitten by a poisonous snake"? Those risks are real, but who stays away from picnics because of them? We have built-in defense mechanisms in our own minds to shield us from the clear and present dangers that are everywhere. A person may have an accurate assessment of real danger but still be insane because he has lost the normal use of defense mechanisms.

Now apply that idea to the question of guilt. Luther was a guilty man. He understood the law of God like probably no other Christian except the Apostle Paul before him. He knew the severe penalty for breaking the law of God, and he knew that his soul was exposed to the potential torment of everlasting damnation. But most people rationalize and deny their guilt. Most people have a normal defense mechanism to escape any thoughts about the judgment of God. Millions of people go through their whole lives without ever thinking about what's going to happen to them when they stand before a holy God and have to give an account for every idle word they spoke. You see, Luther took those teachings of sacred Scripture very seriously. And the law of God terrified him. And so the question is, Was he crazy? It has been said that there is a fine line between genius and insanity. Perhaps Luther skated back and forth across that line throughout his whole life. In many ways, he was a victim of his own genius.

Luther experienced a couple of moments of crisis that would test his sanity. The first took place when he was to give and celebrate his first Mass as an ordained monk. Between the time of his entrance into the monastery as a novice and the celebration of his first Mass, he was able to mend his fences with his father. Perhaps Margarethe, his mother, pleaded with her husband not to be so harsh with their wayward son, who had chosen the religious life over the prosperous life of law. Hans Luther began bragging to his associates in the business world about his son, the ordained priest. Hans personally invited his closest business associates in the mining business to attend Luther's first Mass. Hans brought his associates to the monastery at Erfurt to witness his son's first Mass, and he had planned a party of celebration afterward.

Early in the Mass, Luther, decked in the garments of a priest, flawlessly went through the order of the liturgy, until he came to that critical moment when the miracle of transubstantiation took place, when the common elements of bread and wine were believed to be supernaturally and miraculously changed into the actual body and blood of Jesus. This supposedly took place during the prayer of consecration. One of the powers vested in the priest at ordination is the power to pray the prayer that God will hear to bring about this amazing miracle. At the moment in the Mass when the prayer of consecration was to be said, Luther opened his mouth to say the words, and nothing came out. He stood frozen at the altar, petrified, beads of sweat on his forehead, a visible tremor in his body, his lip quivering, and he was unable to voice the words. In the midst of this embarrassing moment, one of the other priests stood in, said the prayer for Luther, and enabled the Mass to continue.

Hans Luther was beside himself. He had come to show off his son the priest, and his son had failed in his most holy hour, to the absolute chagrin and embarrassment of his father. Hans challenged Martin's call to the priesthood. Luther essentially said to his father: "Don't you understand? I had the body and blood of Jesus Christ in my hands. How do I as a sinful man handle these holy things? How can I speak normally in the presence of such wonder and awe?" Here was the problem. Luther wasn't crazy. He believed this. He believed that the Lord Jesus Christ was there. He really believed that he was standing on holy ground. Whereas other men in the priesthood went through the motions and did these rituals as a matter of course, Luther was trembling in his humanity to be in the presence of the holy.

Another point of crisis for Luther concerned the practice of pilgrimage. A pilgrimage required a pilgrim to go to a cathedral that had a reliquary, the section of the cathedral where a relic or a collection of relics from antiquity was preserved. Relics were things such as the bones of the Apostles, hair from the beard of John the Baptist, and milk from the breast of the Virgin Mary. Certain cathedrals had massive collections of relics. When people made a pilgrimage to a holy site where they could come in contact with these sacred items, they could receive indulgences and forgiveness of their sins now and in purgatory. The two cities in the world most valuable for pilgrimages were Jerusalem and Rome. Rome was the visible center of the Roman Catholic Church, where one could find the bones of Peter and of Paul. Making the journey from Germany to Rome would be an unbelievable opportunity.

Luther was one of two brothers selected to make this trip for business concerns of their monastery. This selection perhaps gave Luther more joy than any other experience that he had in the monastery. His only regret was that his mother and father were still alive, because he wanted to make the journey to Rome for the benefit of its pilgrimage and to use the indulgences from the trip for his parents. But since they were still alive, he couldn't do that, and so he dedicated the pilgrimage to his grandparents. It took several months to travel from Germany to Rome on foot.

This trip was the most significant disillusionment of Luther's life. When he got to Rome, instead of finding a holy city, he found a city marked by unprecedented corruption. He noticed that the priests in the city did five or six Masses in an hour. They went through the liturgy as fast as they could recite the words and then collect the fees for it. That scandalized this idealistic young monk. Even worse was the sexual behavior of the priests in Rome, who, as a matter of common practice, engaged in the use of prostitutes, both female and male. But for Luther the highlight of the pilgrimage was visiting the Lateran church, which had been the main church of Rome before St. Peter's was built. The Lateran church housed the Sacred Steps. These are the steps that the Crusaders recovered when they went to Jerusalem. The steps had led to the judgment hall where Jesus was judged by Pontius Pilate. History records that these were the steps on which our Lord actually went up and down. The Crusaders dismantled the entire staircase in Jerusalem and brought it back to Rome. It became a focal point for indulgences. Pilgrims would go up the steps on their hands and knees and recite an Our Father or a Hail Mary on each step until they got to the top, and then they would receive the indulgences from this pilgrimage.

When I first visited Rome, the place I wanted to visit more than anywhere else was the Lateran church to see whether the sacred steps were still there. They were. I wanted to walk up them just because I wanted to see where Luther had had this crisis. But I couldn't get near the stairs. They were covered with pilgrims on their hands and knees, and a large sign next to the stairs explained how many indulgences were available. So this practice that Luther witnessed is still going on. Luther himself went through the process of climbing up the stairs on his knees, kissing each stair, saying the rosary, and so on. When he got to the top, he stood up, and he said aloud to no one in particular, "Who knows if it is true?" The doubt that was cast in his heart and that pierced his soul that day would not be relieved until another crisis occurred five years later.

3

Tower
Experience

As we have seen, the young Martin Luther had a propensity for experiencing a serious crisis every five years. In 1505, he had the lightning-bolt experience that led him to enter the monastery. In 1510, he experienced disillusionment on his journey and pilgrimage to Rome. But perhaps the most significant crisis of his life, the episode that defined him as a man, as a theologian, as a Reformer, and as a Christian, occurred in 1515, in what has been called his tower experience. But before we look at the tower experience, we have to learn how Luther got from Erfurt to Wittenberg.

Shortly after he returned from his experience in Rome, he was called to move from Erfurt to the Augustinian cloister of the village of Wittenberg. Now, Erfurt was a major city in Germany with a major university, and Wittenberg was a small village of about two thousand inhabitants, and the city was less than one mile long. The name *Wittenberg* means "white hill" or "white little mountain." The village was situated on a stretch of white sand, and it bordered the Elbe River. Wittenberg's significance at this time in history was that it had been established by Frederick the Wise, also known as Frederick, Elector of Saxony. Frederick the Wise was one of the major players of the Protestant Reformation, though his involvement was largely unintentional. Frederick's dream was to create a cultural and intellectual center in Wittenberg that would rival the university at Heidelberg and the other great intellectual centers of Germany. To that end, he scoured the German countryside, asking various monasteries to nominate their finest young scholars to join his new faculty at Wittenberg, and he was able to procure the services of three brilliant young scholars, one of whom was Martin Luther. Luther had not yet completed his doctor's degree. He had his master's in biblical studies, and he was summoned to Wittenberg to be the professor of Bible on the faculty there.

In addition to founding the university at Wittenberg, Frederick also wanted to create the finest reliquary in Germany. His dream was to make Wittenberg the Rome of Germany, and so over a period of about ten years, he searched far and wide to collect various relics that would attract pilgrims from all over Europe. He amassed a collection of more than nineteen thousand relics, whose total indulgence value was 1,902,202 years plus about seven months' worth of time relieved from purgatory. So Frederick's dream of establishing a giant reliquary in Wittenberg was accomplished. The collection of relics included a piece of straw from the manger of Jesus, hair from Jesus' beard, a piece of the cross, a piece of stone from the Mount of Ascension, and even a branch from the burning bush of Moses. This was quite a collection.

Frederick the Wise is called elector of Saxony because he was one of several men in Europe who had a vote in the selection of the Holy Roman emperor, the man who would preside over the Holy Roman Empire. In 1519, Emperor Maximilian I died, the throne was left vacant, and three candidates stood to succeed Maximilian. Two were the front-runners, and the third was a dark horse. The front-runners were Francis, who was the king of France at the time, and Charles, who was the king of Spain. The third candidate was the king of England, Henry VIII. The pope at this time, Leo X, desperately did not want either Francis or Charles to become the new emperor of the Holy Roman Empire. So he tried to lobby Frederick to throw his hat into the ring and run for the office of emperor. To that end, Leo X honored Frederick by giving him the highest honor that the pope could give a secular ruler, the Order of the Golden Rose. He bestowed the honor on Frederick, hoping that it would induce Frederick to seek the emperorship of the Holy Roman Empire. Frederick, however, declined. He was not interested in running for emperor and, in fact, cast one of the deciding votes that put Charles on the throne as emperor of the Holy Roman Empire.

In addition to wisely bringing Luther to Wittenberg, where the Reformation began, Frederick served as Luther's protector during the critical years. Historians have said that if it weren't for the influence of Frederick the Wise, Luther would certainly have been hunted down and executed. Even though Frederick remained loyal to the Roman Catholic Church, he was also loyal to his faculty, and he wanted to make sure that Luther wasn't unjustly persecuted or prosecuted and executed, so Frederick stood in his defense for many years.

When Luther came to Wittenberg as a professor of Bible, he began his lectures in 1513, giving lengthy lectures on the book of Psalms. One thing we often overlook about Luther is that he was a master linguist and an outstanding interpreter of sacred Scripture. In fact, as his method of biblical interpretation matured, it changed the whole shape of biblical interpretation from the Middle Ages to modern approaches to Scripture. In the Middle Ages, the favorite means of interpreting the Bible was through the use of the quadriga. The quadriga was a fourfold method of interpreting the Bible. First, a person looked at the literal sense of a text. Then he found the ethical meaning of the text. Then he found the mystical meaning of the text, and finally he found the allegorical meaning of the text. This method led to all kinds of wild speculation and imaginative interpretations of the Bible, to such an extent that Luther said that under that system the Bible became a nose of wax; anybody could twist and distort it to make it fit whatever theory one wanted to bring to the Scriptures.

Luther gradually came to the position that the proper method of interpreting Scripture was by finding what he called the *sensus literalis*, the literal sense. What Luther meant by the *sensus literalis* was that we are to interpret the Bible according to how it is written. If it's historical narrative, you interpret it according to the rules of historical narrative; if it's poetry, you interpret it according to the rules of poetry; if it's didactic, you interpret it according to those canons; and so on. A noun is a noun and a verb is a verb, and you are to treat the Bible, in that sense, as you would any other book. Now, of course, it's not like any other book because it is the Word of God, but nevertheless Luther built a hedge around all attempts to have a mythical, spiritualized interpretation of the Word of God. He wanted to look for the plain sense and meaning of Scripture, and understand the Word of God as it had originally been written and given. He developed this principle of biblical interpretation during his teaching years at Wittenberg, beginning with his lengthy exposition of the book of Psalms.

Luther's most significant crisis, the tower experience, began when he was given the task of lecturing on the book of Romans. He began by reading through the first chapter, and he came to Romans 1:16: "For I am not ashamed of the gospel, for it is the power of God for salvation to everyone who believes, to the Jew first and also to the Greek." And then in verse 17, which most scholars grant to be the thematic statement for the entire epistle of Romans, Paul writes, "For in it [the gospel] the righteousness of God is revealed from faith for faith, as it is written, 'The righteous shall live by faith.'" Verse 17 spoke of the subject that terrified Luther more than any other—namely, the righteousness of God. That is why he had worked so hard in the monastery, being so rigorous in his asceticism, in his pilgrimages, and with his confessions. Luther knew that if God judged Luther according to God's standard of righteousness, then Luther would perish. He also understood that no matter how hard he tried and no matter what he did, he would never be able to satisfy the demands of God's justice or God's righteousness in order to make his way into heaven. So the ultimate barrier that stood between Luther and his God was the righteousness of God.

Luther understood in the deepest part of his soul the chasm that exists between the righteousness of God and the unrighteousness of the sinner, and he saw no possible way to bridge the gap. But as he read Romans 1 and prepared his lectures, he came to a completely new and radical understanding of what Paul was saying in verse 17. Luther was stopped short. He asked himself: "What does it mean that there's a righteousness that is from faith to faith? What does it mean that the righteous shall live by faith?" As understanding began to dawn on Luther, he realized that Paul was speaking of a righteousness that God in his grace was making available to those who would receive it passively, not those who would achieve it actively; they could receive it by faith and thereby be reconciled to a holy and righteous God.

There was a linguistic trick going on here too. The Latin word for "justification" that was used at this time in church history was *justificare*. It came from the Roman judicial system, and it was made up of the word *justus*, which is "justice" or "righteousness," and *ficare*, which means "to make." The Latin fathers understood the doctrine of justification as what happens when God, through the sacraments of the church, makes unrighteous people righteous. But Luther was looking now at the Greek word that is in the New Testament, *dikaiosyne*—not the Latin word. The Greek word didn't mean to *make* righteous but rather to *regard as* righteous, to *count as* righteous, to *declare* righteous. This was the moment of awakening for Luther. He said, "You mean here Paul is not talking about the righteousness by which God Himself is righteous, but a righteousness that God freely gives by His grace to people who don't have righteousness of their own?" He also read an essay by Augustine, "On the Spirit and the Letter," in which Augustine affirmed that in Romans, Paul was not talking about God's righteousness but rather was talking about a righteousness that was made available to believers by faith.

And so Luther concluded that the righteousness by which we will be saved is not ours. It's what he called a *justitia alienum*, an alien righteousness, a righteousness that belongs properly to somebody else. It's a righteousness that is *extra nos*, outside us—namely, the righteousness of Christ. Luther said, "When I discovered that, I was born again of the Holy Ghost, and the doors of paradise swung open and I walked through." There's no way to understand Luther's tenacity and unwillingness to compromise on the doctrine of justification by faith alone apart from this life-changing, born-again experience when, for the first time in his life, he understood the gospel and what it means to be redeemed by somebody else's righteousness.

4

Building St. Peter's

Later in life, Martin Luther would say that once he understood the righteousness of God, he began to see it on almost every page of the Bible, and it altered his entire understanding of theology and the Christian life.

Meanwhile, back in Rome, momentous things were happening. Two popes, whom even Roman Catholic historians have described as some of the most corrupt popes in the history of the church, were in power during this time. Julius II, known as the warrior pope, was the head of his soldiers. He spilled volumes of blood as he annexed lands to papal control. Julius II had an ambitious dream. He wanted to build a new cathedral for the Roman bishop, a new basilica with a dome that would cover an enormous church and house the bones of the Apostles Peter and Paul. Soon after the footers were laid for St. Peter's Basilica, Julius II died. He was succeeded by the Medici pope Leo X, who depleted the treasuries of the Roman Catholic Church. The church was on the brink of bankruptcy, and the building of St. Peter's was halted. It seemed that the building of St. Peter's would never be completed.

While Leo X was struggling with depleted finances in Rome, an ambitious young prince in Germany of the Hohenzollern line was trying to rise in power. Though Prince Albert of Brandenburg was too young by canon law to become a bishop, he had already secured two bishoprics, one in Halberstadt and the other in Magdeburg. He acquired these two bishoprics through the practice of simony. Simony was the process by which people bought church offices. They paid the pope or the ecclesiastical structures enough money to be rewarded with the appointments of bishop. The term *simony* is from the book of Acts, which records that the magician Simon Magus tried to purchase the Holy Spirit from Peter when he saw Peter working his miracles (see Acts 8:9–24). Peter replied, "May your silver perish with you," which is a polite translation.

Simony became rampant in the Middle Ages. This is the kind of corruption that Luther witnessed during his critical visit to Rome in 1510. First, you were not allowed to be bishop of more than one place. Second, canon law had an age requirement for all bishops. Albert wasn't old enough, and yet he had not just one but two bishoprics. Albert wanted to be the most powerful cleric in all of Germany. An archbishopric became vacant in the large city of Mainz, and Albert's lust was inflamed. He knew that if he could capture the archbishopric of Mainz along with the other two sees that he already had, he could fulfill his ambition. And so he negotiated with Rome. The pope demanded a payment of twelve thousand gold ducats in exchange for the archbishopric of Mainz. Prince Albert countered with an offer of seven thousand gold ducats. The pope had said he wanted twelve thousand, one thousand for each of the twelve Apostles, and Albert countered with seven thousand, one thousand for each of the seven deadly sins. They reached a compromise of ten thousand gold ducats, a thousand for each of the Ten Commandments.

But Prince Albert didn't have ten thousand gold ducats at his disposal to purchase the archbishopric of Mainz, and so he sought to borrow the money from the Fugger bankers in Germany. They agreed to lend him the funds, which he would then pass on to the pope. The pope gave another benefit to Albert of Brandenburg. He gave Albert permission to lead the distribution of indulgences throughout Germany, in whatever provinces it was politically permitted. Of the funds that Albert would raise through the distribution of papal indulgences, 50 percent was to go to Rome for the building of St. Peter's, and 50 percent was to go to pay off Albert's debt to the German bankers. This began the process of the widespread sale of indulgences in Germany.

To understand how this worked, we need to clarify some things. The Roman Catholic Church believes that as the successor to the Apostle Peter and as a vicar of Christ on earth, the pope possesses the keys of the kingdom. He has what was called the "power of the keys." In Matthew 18:18, Jesus said to the disciples, "Whatever you bind on earth shall be bound in heaven, and whatever you loose on earth shall be loosed in heaven." The Roman Catholic Church believes that Jesus gave the keys of the kingdom not just to the disciples in general but to Peter in particular, and that Petrine authority and ownership of the keys of the kingdom would then pass to all of Peter's successors, all the way down to Leo X. What was so important about the keys of the kingdom? The keys of the kingdom did not access the vault that contained gold ducats; they accessed what the church calls the treasury of merit. The treasury of merit is the depository where all the merits that were earned by Jesus Christ are deposited. In addition to the merits deposited by Jesus, there are also the deposits of the merits of Mary, of Joseph, of the original Apostles, and of the great saints throughout the ages. The treasury of merit is a vast sum of merits that had been amassed through the centuries through the work of Christ, through the work of the Apostles, and through the work of the great saints.

According to the Roman Catholic Church, in order for somebody to go to heaven, a person has to arrive at a state in life in which he is inherently righteous, in which there is not only no mortal sin tarnishing his character or behavioral performance but also no venial sin—no blemish whatsoever. If a person dies with any blemish attached to his soul, before he can get to heaven he must first serve time in purgatory, which is the place of purging. It purges the blemishes from the soul as a crucible purges the dross from pure gold. A person's time in purgatory can range from a few days to millions of years, depending on how much blemish he carries with him into purgatory. And so people who lack merit to get into heaven have to find a way to diminish the time that they spend in this place of purging. Only a handful of people in history have achieved enough merit to go directly to heaven when they die.

The Roman Catholic Church distinguishes among three types of merit. The first is condign merit. Condign merit is so virtuous that it imposes an obligation of justice on God to reward it. If a person possesses that kind of merit, God would be unjust if He didn't give an appropriate reward for it. The church believes that the merit of Jesus was condign merit. But not only did Jesus achieve condign merit; other saints in history did as well. The second type of merit is called congruous merit. Congruous merit is not as high or as meritorious as condign merit. Congruous merit is sufficient to make it fitting or congruous for God to reward it. Congruous merit is a factor in the Roman Catholic Church's doctrine of the sacrament of penance, as well as its doctrine of justification. A third kind of merit is supererogatory merit, which is achieved by works of supererogation. Works of supererogation are meritorious works that are above and beyond the call of duty. They are merits that are achieved beyond what God requires of obedient Christians. For example, martyrs by their martyrdom were able to earn supererogatory merit. And great saints such as Jerome, Francis of Assisi, Augustine, and Thomas Aquinas were so virtuous in life that not only did they acquire enough condign merit to get into heaven directly without having to go through purgatory but they had more merit than they needed to go to heaven. They had a surplus of merit gained through works of supererogation. And the surplus merit earned by the saints is deposited in the treasury of merit.

So we see the picture. This treasury contains the merit of Christ, the merit of the holy family, the merit of the Apostles, and the merit of the saints. And this surplus merit may be distributed at the judgment of the pope, who has the power of the keys. An indulgence is a papal grant by which a certain amount of merit is taken out of the treasury of merit and applied to those who are deficient in merit, so that their time in purgatory will be less. Obtaining indulgences was extremely important then (as it is now) in the Roman system of salvation.

To acquire an indulgence and gain the application of merit from the treasury of merit, certain things had to take place, things that were associated with the sacrament of penance. The sacrament of penance involves the contrite sinner's coming to confession, confessing his sin to the priest, receiving priestly absolution, and then doing certain works of congruous merit, such as saying Hail Marys or Our Fathers or giving restitution. The giving of alms was also part of the sacrament of penance. If a person gave alms out of a genuine sense of repentance, then those alms could gain the transfer of indulgences to his account. The canon law of the church made it clear that this was not to be understood as a crass selling of forgiveness, whereby people could simply pay to get their relatives out of purgatory. But the pope was using this process to gain the finances he needed to build St. Peter's. And this practice in Germany provoked Luther and eventually led him to post the Ninety-Five Theses in 1517.

5

The Indulgence Controversy

After Pope Leo X authorized the sale of indulgences through Roman Catholic lands, he worked out an arrangement with Prince Albert of Brandenburg to sell indulgences in Germany, except where it was illegal, which included the area of Electoral Saxony. Under the authority of Frederick the Wise, the church was not allowed to sell indulgences in that particular territory. But Dominican monk Johann Tetzel supervised the sale of indulgences in other parts of Germany. Tetzel was known for his creative marketing skills. When representatives of the church visited a German town, they entered with great pomp and pageantry. A solemn procession was led by a cross that contained the sign of the pope, as well as a papal bull, which was carried on a gold-embroidered velvet cushion. (A papal bull is an edict written by the pope with his authority by which he communicates something to the church.) People in the village would gather around, and Tetzel would deliver one of his famous sermons. The goal of his sermons was to tug on the heartstrings of the peasants about the predicament that their deceased relatives were experiencing in purgatory. He would say things such as this: "Can you hear their cries? Can you hear them pleading for you this day to get these indulgences to reduce their time in purgatory?" The famous jingle that Tetzel composed translates into English as "Every time a coin in the coffer rings, a soul from purgatory springs."

Though Tetzel was not able to cross into Electoral Saxony, many peasants from the region of Wittenberg made the short journey into the neighboring territory and availed themselves of the opportunity to purchase indulgences for their departed relatives. This particular action infuriated Martin Luther, who was at that time a professor of theology and Bible at the University of Wittenberg. And so Luther wrote down in clear, terse language Ninety-Five Theses of protests against the corruption behind the sale of indulgences. He was chiefly agitated by Tetzel's tactics, which exceeded what was actually authorized by the church. In fact, Prince Albert had made it clear that the value of indulgences depended on a true spirit of contrition by those who purchased them. But this was obscured in Tetzel's marketing techniques. So initially Luther's protest was not against Rome itself but against this agent of the church who Luther was convinced was misrepresenting the church.

Luther wrote his Ninety-Five Theses in Latin, which was the language of the scholars, not the people. On All Hallow's Eve day, Luther walked down the city streets of Wittenberg, accompanied by his friend Johannes Agricola, to the Castle Church, and there he tacked the Ninety-Five Theses on the church door. At that time, the front door of the Castle Church served as a bulletin board for the university. By writing in Latin,

Luther was asking for the faculty of the university to discuss his points behind closed doors. But a couple things occurred that Luther did not expect. First, none of the academicians responded to the invitation. No one showed up to discuss the Ninety-Five Theses. But second, some enterprising students who could read Latin saw the theses tacked to the door, realized their significance, and, without Luther's knowledge or permission, had the theses translated into German. Taking advantage of the recent invention of the printing press by Johannes Gutenberg, they printed thousands of copies; it was said that within two weeks the Ninety-Five Theses could be found in every village in Germany.

Theologian Karl Barth commented that what happened here was something like a blind man climbing a ladder in a church tower. When he loses his footing, he reaches out for anything he can find to help stabilize him, and his hand grabs hold of a rope. Unbeknownst to the blind man, the rope is attached to the church bell, and in his innocence he awakens everybody in the town. The last thing that Luther wanted or expected to do was to start a protest or a reformation. He wanted to look at the theological issues inherent in the whole question of indulgences. Luther had a high view of the church and of the papacy. Despite the disillusionment he experienced in 1510 during his pilgrimage to Rome, he nevertheless wanted to be a dutiful son of the church. And so he next wrote an exposition, in much calmer language, of each of the theses and sent several copies to Prince Albert. At the same time, Tetzel sent his arguments to Albert and complained about Luther's interference in the collection of the revenue from indulgences. Albert was not mollified by Luther's gentle exposition, and he sent copies of Luther's exposition of the theses to Rome and to the pope in protest against Luther.

At the time, there was some competition in Germany between the Dominican monastic order and the Augustinian monastic order; Tetzel represented the Dominicans and Luther the Augustinians. When the pope looked at the theses, his initial response, according to some historians, was something like this: "Ah, this is just the work of a drunken German monk. He'll get over it in the morning." But Luther didn't get over it in the morning, and the issue began to mushroom. In 1518, Tetzel wrote his own theses in response to Luther's, and he sent them to Wittenberg. The students there at the university burned these theses. Some people were demanding that Luther be summoned to Rome to be tried for heresy, and the pope himself was so inclined. But Frederick the Wise interceded on Luther's behalf and influenced the pope to relinquish the order to bring Luther to Rome.

Luther continued to request a theological discussion in which he could engage the church representatives in debate over the issues raised by the Ninety-Five Theses. One of the ironies of the theses is that they contain nothing about the doctrine of justification, the topic that later became the center of the Reformation. The emphasis of the theses concerned indulgences and the doctrine of the treasury of merit. Luther complained that Tetzel was bypassing the sober call for true contrition and replacing it with attrition. And that distinction is one for us to be aware of at all times. Attrition is repentance that is motivated out of a fear of punishment or as a ticket out of hell, whereas contrition is repentance that is motivated by a deeply felt, serious sorrow and recognition of having offended God by our sins. Luther was an expert in the experience of contrition, since he had spent so much time involved in it in the monastery. Luther saw the indulgence movement as a cheapening of forgiveness and a cheapening of an understanding of the grace of God.

Between the posting of Luther's theses in 1517 and the Diet of Worms in 1521, Luther was involved in three significant meetings. The first took place in 1518 in Heidelberg, Germany. The occasion was a dispute over philosophy and theology between the Augustinians and the Dominicans. The purpose of the debate in Heidelberg was not to discuss the theses. But Luther was asked to attend, representing the Augustinian faculty from Wittenberg. In Luther's discussion defending Wittenberg's Augustinian professors, he set forth some of the most important concepts of his own theology that were developing even at this early time; he made a distinction between what is called the *theologia crucis* and the *theologia gloriae*—that is, a theology of the cross and a theology of glory. He felt that the church had gotten caught up with her own self-exaltation and a triumphant spirit. Luther said that the gospel is a theology of the cross. And only when we come to grips with the cross will we understand what Christianity is all about. In that particular meeting, Luther was exceedingly winsome and brilliant in his presentation, and those in attendance were amazed at his manner of dealing with controversial issues.

In contrast to the usual image we have of Luther as being somewhat bombastic and harsh, a Dominican friar who was present at that Heidelberg meeting presents a different side of Luther: "Their wiles were not able to move him an inch. ... His sweetness in answering is remarkable. His patience in listening is incomparable. In his explanations you would recognize the acumen of Paul, not Scotus: his answers, so brief, so wise and drawn from the Scriptures, easily made all hearers his admirers."[*] I find that observation of Luther's demeanor interesting. But what interests

_____

[*]   Gordon Rupp, *Luther's Progress to the Diet of Worms* (New York: Harper & Row, 1964), 56–57.

me more than the observation is the man from whose pen these words came. These words were written by a young Dominican scholar named Martin Bucer. Bucer would later influence another young Roman Catholic theologian: John Calvin.

After Heidelberg, largely through the intercession of Frederick the Wise, the Roman Catholic Church authorized two more meetings, one in Augsburg and another in Leipzig, where Luther would have the opportunity to engage in debate.

6

Progress
to Worms

Martin Luther's visit to Heidelberg won many more people in Germany to the Lutheran cause. But the next great crisis took place the same year, 1518. Rather than Luther's going to Rome to be tried for heresy, Rome came to Germany in the person of its most able theologian, Cardinal Thomas Cajetan. Luther was promised safe conduct if he would meet with Cajetan in Augsburg. Some of Luther's friends urged him not to go, fearing that he would be betrayed and carried off to Rome to be burned at the stake as a heretic. But Luther wanted to go to Augsburg because this was his wish come true. He would finally have the opportunity to reasonably debate with the princes of the church.

In Augsburg, Luther had four interviews with Cardinal Cajetan, and they did not go as Luther had hoped. Instead of inviting an open discussion and debate, the cardinal insisted that Luther repent, recant his teachings, and promise that he would never teach these things again. Luther grew more and more frustrated as Cajetan became more and more angry. Historians say that Cajetan got the best of Luther because he was able to maneuver Luther into taking a position that clearly brought him into conflict with the Roman Catholic Church. Much of their discussion in Augsburg focused on the treasury of merit and the issue of indulgences that Luther had challenged in his Ninety-Five Theses. Cajetan, armed with the knowledge of church history, pointed out to Luther that in 1300 Pope Boniface VIII had authorized, by papal authority, the principle of indulgences and their sale. And later in 1343, Pope Clement VI in his papal encyclical *Unigenitus Dei Filius* had developed and authorized the doctrine of the treasury of merit. So Cajetan was able to show that

Luther's antagonism toward the treasury of merit and the sale of indulgences was in conflict with two historical popes. Luther pointed out that these doctrines were not in the Bible; he dared to challenge the authority of the popes in these matters, saying that the popes had simply erred.

The doctrine of papal infallibility had not yet been officially decreed. That would not come until the nineteenth century, at the First Vatican Council in 1870 under Pope Pius IX. But just because the church did not declare papal infallibility until 1870 does not mean that it believed in papal infallibility for first time in 1870. It just then became a formal doctrine of the church. Tradition had always maintained the idea of papal infallibility, and Luther was in direct conflict with two popes. Cajetan became so angry with him that Luther was barely able to escape from Augsburg with his life and return to Wittenberg.

The next disputation occurred in 1519 at Leipzig. Luther met with Johann Eck, the chief Roman Catholic theologian in Germany. Now, this debate took a different course from the one in Augsburg. Eck brought up teachings of the Bohemian Reformer from a hundred years earlier, Jan Hus. Eck indicated that certain doctrines for which Hus had been condemned and burned at the stake were similar to Luther's teachings. Hus had argued that the ultimate authority of the Christian church and the only authority that could bind the Christian conscience was holy Scripture, the Word of God. And Luther, after challenging the authority of the pope at Augsburg, was now sounding the same message. Just as Cajetan had maneuvered Luther into admitting that he differed with two popes in history, now Eck in his own brilliant way was able to get Luther to admit that he held beliefs similar to those of Hus—beliefs for which Hus had been condemned to death not just by a pope but by a church council. In Leipzig, Eck maneuvered Luther to say that popes and church councils can make mistakes.

Now Luther had laid his ax at the root of both the tree of the papacy and the tree of the authority of church councils. He was now called the German Hus. The following year, in 1520, Leo X issued a papal bull, condemning Martin Luther as a heretic. All the papal encyclicals (letters from the pope) are named for their opening words in Latin. The name of this papal bull was *Exsurge Domine*, which means "Rise up, O Lord." To paraphrase, it says, "Rise up, O Lord; there is a wild boar loose in your vineyard." Then, "Rise up, St. Peter; there's somebody challenging your authority." And later, "Rise up, St. Paul." The pope called for Christ and the Apostles to rise up against Luther.

Luther's works had made their way to Rome and had been publicly burned in St. Peter's Square. It took three months for the papal bull to reach Wittenberg, and when it did, Luther burned it in a bonfire. The game was now afoot, and there was no turning back.

At this point, the authorities of the Holy Roman Empire were also engaging in these issues. Before he died, Emperor Maximilian was outraged at the furor that this Lutheran revolt had created throughout not just Germany, but other countries in the Holy Roman Empire. But before he could do anything about it, he died and was replaced by Charles of Spain. As we saw in chapter 3, Pope Leo X wanted Frederick, Elector of Saxony, to be the new Holy Roman Emperor instead of either Francis of France or Charles of Spain. In fact, in the first ballot, the electors chose neither Francis nor Charles. They elected Frederick. But Frederick turned them down and gave his support to Charles, who then became emperor.

Charles wanted no uprisings in the church, so he called an imperial diet or council. An imperial diet was called for 1521 in the German city of Worms. The emperor summoned Luther to the diet and assured him of safe conduct. Once again, somewhat naively, Luther expected to stand before the church and give a reasoned defense of his writings. His friends, however, didn't trust the emperor or the authorities of Rome, who would be represented at Worms, and they strongly urged Luther not to go, even with the safe conduct. Luther's friends warned him that the town would be filled with devils, every one of them out to get him. Now, Luther was well acquainted with Satan. He wrote about experiencing what he called the *Anfechtung*, the relentless assault of Satan against him. But he was convinced of the truth of his teaching, which now included the doctrine of justification by faith alone, and he had to defend these things publicly. He said to his friends, "If there are as many devils in Worms as there are orange tiles on the roofs of the town, I'm going." Now, virtually every house in eastern Germany has an orange-tiled roof. But Luther and a couple of his friends journeyed from Wittenberg to Worms, and they did so in a covered wagon that was moved on two wheels. This was quite an awkward conveyance.

Luther was apprehensive about what would be waiting for him when he got to Worms. He did not expect that for miles outside the city of Worms, the streets would be lined with peasants shouting and cheering and rooting for Luther. Seeing how much popularity Luther had gained made the authorities nervous. When Luther arrived at the diet and entered the great hall where the emperor and the papal legates were seated, he was not given the opportunity to debate. An interrogator named Eck was also there (this was not the same Eck who had debated him in Leipzig).

In the middle of the hall stood a table piled with the books and pamphlets that Luther had produced in just a very short time. The interrogator asked Luther, "Are these your books?" And he said, "Yes." Then Eck said to him, "You must say before the authorities assembled here today, *Revoco*," which means "I recant." Luther commented that he had written on all kinds of subjects, many of which were not at all in conflict with the classic teaching of the Roman Catholic Church. He wanted to know the specific issues they had with him. Eck pressed him again to simply say *Revoco*, and to say it "without horns"—that is, without deceit. The room became hushed, and Luther answered Eck inaudibly. Eck asked him to repeat himself. Luther requested twenty-four hours to consider, and it was granted him.

That night in his monastic cell, awaiting his fate, Luther wrote a poignant prayer:

> O God, Almighty God everlasting! how dreadful is the world! behold how its mouth opens to swallow me up, and how small is my faith in thee! … Oh! the weakness of the flesh, and the power of Satan! If I am to depend upon any strength of this world—all is over. … The knell is struck.

... Sentence is gone forth. ... O God! O God! O thou, my God! help me against all the wisdom of this world. Do this, I beseech thee; thou shouldst do this ... by thy own mighty power. ... The work is not mine, but thine. I have no business here. ... I have nothing to contend for with these great men of the world! I would gladly pass my days in happiness and peace. But the cause is thine. ... And it is righteous and everlasting! O Lord! help me! O faithful and unchangeable God! I lean not upon man. It were vain! Whatever is of man is tottering, whatever proceeds from him must fail. My God! my God! does thou not hear? My God! art thou no longer living? Nay, thou canst not die. Thou dost but hide thyself. Thou hast chosen me for this work. I know it! ... Therefore, O God, accomplish thine own will! Forsake me not, for the sake of thy well-beloved Son, Jesus Christ, my defense, my buckler, and my stronghold. Lord—where art thou? ... My God, where art thou? ... Come! I pray thee, I am ready. ... Behold me prepared to lay down my life for thy truth ... suffering like a lamb.

For the cause is holy. It is thine own! . . . I will not let thee go! no, nor yet for all eternity! And though the world should be thronged with devils—and this body, which is the work of thine hands, should be cast forth, trodden under foot, cut in pieces, . . . consumed to ashes, my soul is thine. Yes, I have thine own word to assure me of it. My soul belongs to thee, and will abide with thee forever! Amen! O God send help! . . . Amen![*]

The next day he entered the assembly hall, and was again commanded to recant, to say *Revoco*. Luther said: "Since you've asked me to respond plainly and without horns, I will do so. Unless I'm convinced by sacred Scripture or by evident reason, I cannot recant, for my conscience is held captive by the Word of God, and to act against conscience is neither right nor safe. Here I stand. I can do no other. God help me." That was the watershed of the Protestant Reformation. At

---

[*] Quoted in R.C. Sproul, *The Holiness of God* (Wheaton, Ill.: Tyndale, 1985), chapter 5.

those words the audience exploded in fury and confusion. As Luther was leaving the hall, his friends staged a fake kidnapping, and they whisked him off deep into the forest to Wartburg Castle. There he would work for a year, translating the New Testament into German in disguise as a knight, Sir Jörg.

7

The Roman Catholic View of Justification, Part 1

When Protestants are asked why they are Protestant rather than Roman Catholic, many will say that they don't believe they need to confess their sins to a priest, or they don't believe the pope is infallible, or they don't believe in the bodily assumption of the Virgin Mary into heaven. After Desiderius Erasmus wrote his diatribe against Martin Luther, Luther thanked Erasmus for not attacking him on matters that Luther considered to be trivial but rather for addressing the very heart of the issue of the Reformation, which was the question, How does a sinner find salvation in Christ? Luther asserted that the doctrine of justification by faith alone is the article on which the church stands or falls, and that this issue touches the very core of the biblical teaching of salvation. And so we don't want to get bogged down in extraneous issues that could have perhaps been resolved with further meetings and discussions, but we want to focus on this one issue. It is the point over which Christendom was severely fractured and remains fragmented even to this day.

Part of the problem of the doctrine of justification and the distinction between historic Protestantism and Roman Catholicism has to do with the meaning of the word *justification* itself. The English word *justification* is derived from the Latin *justificare*, which etymologically and originally meant "to make righteous." The early Latin fathers, who studied the Latin Vulgate Bible rather than the original Greek New Testament, developed their doctrine of justification based on their understanding of the legal system of the Roman Empire, which used the word *justificare*, "to make righteous." As the church developed that doctrine, the idea of justification came to address the question of how an unrighteous person, such as a fallen sinner, is able to be made righteous. In Rome, the idea emerged that justification occurs after sanctification. That is, to be made just, we first have to be sanctified to the point that we exhibit a righteousness that is acceptable to God.

But the Protestant Reformation focused on the Greek concept of justification, which was derived from the word *dikaioō*, which means "to declare righteous," not "to make righteous." And in Protestantism, justification was understood to come before the process of sanctification. So early on, there was a different understanding of the order of salvation between the two communions. From the Roman Catholic perspective, justification occurs primarily through the use of the sacraments, starting with the sacrament of baptism. So the first step in justification, according to Rome, is the sacrament of baptism. The sacrament of baptism, among others, is said to operate by Rome *ex opere operato*, which means "through the working of the work."

Protestants have understood this to mean that baptism works, as it were, automatically; if a person is baptized, that person is *ex opere operato* placed in a state of grace or in the state of justification. The Roman Catholic communion does not like to use the word *automatic*, because they say that the recipients of baptism must have a certain predisposition; they must at least have no hostility toward the reception of the sacrament for it to function. But Rome has a high view of the efficacy of baptism to bring about the change of the person's status into that of being placed into a state of grace, because in the sacrament of baptism grace is said to be infused.

If you were to press Roman Catholic theologians to define what they mean by *grace*, they would be careful not to define it simply as some kind of substance, spiritual or material, but the language of their sacramental theology uses quantitative terms of grace, that you can have an increase in this infused grace or a diminution. You can lose some of this substantial infused grace, which they say inhabits or resides in the soul. In contrast, Protestants describe grace as an unmerited action of God of benevolence and charity toward people. Now, we do believe in being filled by the Holy Spirit, but that's not quite the same thing. Roman Catholicism teaches that the grace and the righteousness of Christ are poured or infused into the soul of the person at baptism, and that the person is then in a state of grace, at least conditionally. For that justifying grace to be ultimately efficacious, the person who receives it must assent to that infusion of grace and cooperate with that grace.

At the Council of Trent in the sixteenth century when the Roman Catholic Church defined its position over against the protests of the Reformers, it used the term *cooperare et assentare*, to cooperate with and assent to the grace that is being bestowed in the sacrament of baptism. If a person assents to the infusion of grace and cooperates with that infusion, then that person is in a state of grace and a state of justification. Yet the justification that is received through the infusion of Christ's righteousness is by no means immutable. It can change, and the grace that has been received in the sacrament of baptism may be lost. In fact, it may be lost entirely, removing the person from a state of justification and placing him under the threat of damnation. A loss of saving grace occurs when the person commits a particular type of sin. The Roman Catholic Church calls this a mortal sin. Mortal sin is distinguished from venial sin. Venial sin is real sin, but it is less serious than mortal sin.

For example, Roman Catholic moral theology makes distinctions with respect to drinking. Drinking alcohol is not a sin inherently. To get tipsy is a venial sin. To get drunk is a mortal sin. Some moral theologians have even taught that to miss Mass is a mortal sin. There is no absolute universal agreement as to what constitutes mortal sin in the Roman Catholic Church, but many catalogs have been produced throughout the church's history that delineate various sins. Mortal sin is called mortal because it is serious enough to cause the death of the justifying grace that was infused into the person at baptism. The Reformers believed that we find descriptions of greater and lesser sin in the teaching of Jesus. But John Calvin would say that all sin is mortal in that it deserves death. In creation, the threat given to

Adam and Eve was that the soul that sins shall die, and that even the smallest peccadillo is serious enough to be an act of treason against God's sovereign rule and is a serious matter and deserves death. But Calvin would go on to say that though every sin is mortal in the sense that it deserves death, no sin is mortal in the sense that it destroys the saving grace that a Christian receives at his justification.

This distinction between mortal and venial sin was a significant part of the struggle in the sixteenth century. What happens if a person who has been baptized and has therefore received the infusion of the grace of justification, the infused righteousness of Jesus, commits mortal sin and destroys that justifying grace? The Roman church had an antidote to that situation, how a person could be restored to the status of justification in the sight of God. That antidote also comes via a sacrament: the sacrament of penance. The Roman church in the sixteenth century defined the sacrament of penance as the "second plank" of justification after someone has made shipwreck of his faith. Those who made shipwreck of their faith committed mortal sin and lost the grace of justification. But happily, these people can be restored through the sacrament of penance. And as we have seen, the sacrament of penance was at the heart of the indulgence problem. Penance had several elements, not the least of which was confession involving an act of contrition, showing and demonstrating that your confession was moved not merely by a fear of punishment but by a genuine sorrow for having offended God. The confession and contrition is then followed by priestly absolution, whereby the priest says to the penitent person: "*Te absolvo*. I absolve you."

Today, many of the guns of Protestantism are aimed at the ritual elements of the Roman Catholic Church. We hear people say: "I don't need a priest to tell me that I'm absolved of my sin. I don't have to confess my sins to a priest. I can confess directly to God. I don't need the mediation of the saints." But not all the Reformers were opposed to confession. The Lutherans carried on the act of confession because they believed, as the New Testament says, that we are to confess our sins to one another (see James 5:16). They believe it's salutary for Christians to confess their sins to somebody in a situation in which their confession will be protected by the discretion of the minister, and the minister has the authority to declare the assurance of pardon to those who are genuinely sorry for their sins. Many Protestant churches include a corporate confession of sin during the worship service, after which an assurance of pardon is given.

For the Reformers, confession wasn't the issue. The issue was the second step in the sacrament of penance. To be restored to the state of grace, one had to perform works of satisfaction. Here's where works come in. Often Protestants will say that the difference between us and Roman Catholics is that we believe that justification is by faith and that Roman Catholics believe it's by works. We believe that it's by grace; Roman Catholics say that it's by merit. We believe that it's by Christ; they believe that it's through your own self-righteousness. That's a terrible slander against Rome because Rome now and in the sixteenth century and always has said that justification requires faith and the grace of God, and that justification requires the work of Jesus Christ.

The dispute is over that little word *alone*, because for Rome, you must have faith plus works. You must have grace plus merit. You must have Christ plus inherent righteousness in yourself. It was these pluses that became so problematic in the sixteenth century, particularly with respect to that element of the sacrament of penance whereby the penitent has to perform works of satisfaction. The required works may be as simple as saying a number of Our Fathers or a number of Hail Marys. Or one might be required to give restitution to your neighbor after having sinned against him, or going on a pilgrimage, or giving alms.

Rome distinguishes between different kinds of merit. In chapter 4, we examined Rome's distinction between condign merit and congruous merit. Condign merit is so meritorious that it demands a reward. God would be unjust if He did not reward works that were condign. The merit that is acquired through the works of satisfaction in the sacrament of penance do not rise to the level of condign merit. They are considered congruous merit. It is real merit, but it is merit that depends on previous grace; it is merit that simply makes it congruous or fitting for God to restore the person to the state of grace. So in other words, if a person went through the sacrament of penance and did the works of satisfaction prescribed by the priests, then it would be unfitting or incongruous for God not to restore that person to a state of justification.

Martin Luther saw the New Testament teaching of justification by faith alone as a thunderbolt against any kind of merit, condign or congruous. He understood that people should never think that any work they do can in any way add to the satisfaction for our sins that has been accomplished by Christ and by Christ alone.

But we have to explore more deeply the role of faith, particularly in relation to justification. We will examine that topic in the next chapter.

8

The Roman Catholic View of Justification, Part 2

When the theological issue of justification exploded in the sixteenth century, the Roman Catholic Church responded by calling an ecumenical council at the city of Trento (or Trent) in Italy. When we examine the statements of the Council of Trent, we get a look at the official, formal decrees of the Roman Catholic communion with respect to its doctrine of justification.

One thing to note is that many people today believe

that the Reformation is over, and that the decrees of the Council of Trent are not relevant to ecumenical discussions today between Roman Catholic and Protestant representatives. But the Council of Trent was an ecumenical council carrying all the weight of the infallibility of the church. And Rome suffers from a kind of theological hemophilia—if you scratch her theologically, she bleeds to death. So there's a certain sense that Rome, to maintain her triumphant view of the authority of the church and of tradition, cannot repeal the decrees of the Council of Trent. As recently as the Roman Catholic catechism at the end of the twentieth century, we saw a clear reaffirmation of the authority of the Council of Trent. So those who argue that the Tridentine teaching of justification is no longer relevant are simply ignoring what the Roman Catholic Church itself teaches. When I speak about the church, I'm talking about the Roman community. Some priests in America and in places such as Holland and Germany dispute some of the orthodox teachings of their own communion, but as far as the Roman Curia is concerned, the Council of Trent stands immutable on the teaching on justification.

The Council of Trent was held over several sessions, and different issues were addressed at different sessions; for example, the issue of the sacraments was discussed in the first session and the issue of Scripture in the fourth session. Problems pertaining to the corruption of the clergy, such as simony, were brought to the church and addressed at the council. But it is the sixth session of the Council of Trent that has the most relevance to the discussion of the doctrine of justification. That session is divided into two parts. The formal teaching of the Roman Catholic view of justification is one section, and that is followed by the canons, which have to do with the church's repudiation of error and heresy. The canons all follow the formula, "If anyone says . . . , let him be anathema."

The first three canons are directed against Pelagianism, which had been condemned at earlier church councils and were not particularly aimed at the Protestant Reformation. A careful examination of the canons of Trent reveals that in many cases when Rome aimed its guns at the Reformers, it missed the Reformers altogether. The council's anathemas reveal certain misunderstandings. Some therefore say that the council was a result of misunderstanding and that the two sides were talking past each other without really understanding the issues. Unfortunately, that may be true to a degree, but not completely. Some of the canons are right on the mark, and they do clearly anathematize the Reformation doctrine of justification by faith. Here is the significance of that. If the Reformation articulation of the biblical doctrine of justification is correct, then to anathematize it is to anathematize the gospel. Any communion or organization that claims to be Christian but denies or condemns an essential truth of Christianity becomes apostate and is no longer a true or valid church.

That is part of the problem with the ongoing discussions between Roman Catholic and Protestant bodies. Many Protestant bodies don't care about doctrinal differences, and they're happy to enter into discussions and ecumenical agreements with Rome. But if one takes the biblical doctrine of justification seriously, on that point there can be no rapprochement. There cannot be any unity unless one side or the other surrenders, because the two positions are incompatible. At some point, we must choose which one is right. Somebody is right and somebody is wrong, and whoever is wrong has significantly distorted the New Testament gospel. As the Apostle Paul wrote to the Galatians, "If anyone is preaching to you a gospel contrary to the one you received, let him be accursed" (Gal. 1:9). He says that even if it is an angel from heaven, "let him be accursed" (v. 8). So somebody is under the anathema or curse of God here, and that issue has not been resolved.

As we noted, the sixth session of Trent has two parts. The more difficult element to resolve is found in the first part, in which the Roman Catholic doctrine is itself defined. Rome goes to great lengths to define what saving faith is and what saving faith involves. As we saw in chapter 7, it is a slanderous caricature to say that we believe in justification by faith and that Rome simply believes that justification is by works, as though faith were not necessary. In truth, Rome clearly teaches in the sixth session of Trent that faith is what we call a "necessary condition" for justification. For Rome, faith involves three elements or steps. The sixth session speaks of faith as the *initium*, the *fundamentum*, and the *radix* of justification. This means first that faith is the initiation of justification. It's the starting place, that which begins the process of justification. Second, faith is the foundation, the fundamental structure, on which justification is established; without that foundation, there can be no justification. Third, faith is the root, the radical core, of justification. It is important that we understand that for Rome, faith is no mere appendage to justification. It's not some insignificant plus that is added to the sacramental power of the church. Rather, faith initiates, is the foundation of, and is the radical core for justification, and so it is a necessary condition. This means that it's a condition without which justification cannot follow.

The difference, however, is that according to Rome, faith is not a sufficient condition. A sufficient condition is one that, if it is met, will surely issue in the desired result. Oxygen, for example, is in most cases a necessary condition for fire. But it's not a sufficient condition. You need oxygen to have fire, but you can have oxygen and still not have fire, because it doesn't have sufficient power to cause a fire. We know that the Council of Trent teaches that faith is not sufficient in and of itself to yield the result of justification, because in its treatment of the loss of justification through mortal sin, it explicitly declares that a person can have his faith intact and, while in a state of faith, can commit mortal sin. And when you commit mortal sin while in a posture of true faith, faith is not lost, but justification is. In that instance, one can have what we would call saving faith without justification. You can retain the faith but lose the justification because you have committed mortal sin.

The next point that we have to understand is what the Roman Catholic Church understands to be the instrumental cause of justification. When we speak of things that cause other things, we generally think of causality in simple one-dimensional terms, but the Roman Catholic Church distinguishes among several different types of causes. This goes back to the medieval synthesis between Roman Catholic theology and the philosophy of the ancient Greek Aristotle. When Aristotle contemplated the mystery of motion (what moves one thing to cause another to produce change and mutations), he examined what he called various types of causes. Aristotle's famous illustration had to do with the making of a statue by a sculptor. He defined the *material cause* as that out of which something is made. You can't have a sculpture of stone without stone. The matter out of which that beautiful sculpture is formed is the stone. Then Aristotle talked about the *formal cause*. If the artist first sketched what he envisioned the final statue as looking like, then that would be his blueprint, that would be the format he would follow, the formal cause. The final cause would be the purpose for which the statue was being made. Maybe it was being made to beautify somebody's garden, and that's why the sculptor was hired to make the sculpture. The *efficient cause*, the cause that actually transforms the matter into a beautiful statue, would be the work of the sculptor himself. He is the efficient cause.

Aristotle also spoke about the *instrumental cause*, the instrument or the tools that are used to bring about a change. A sculptor doesn't approach a block of marble with a picture of what he wants to see and then simply command it to be a statue. A sculptor has to take his hammer and chisel and begin to chip away at that block of stone in order to shape it into a piece of art. The utensils that he uses are called the instrumental cause of bringing the statue into existence.

The Roman Catholic Church used that kind of metaphor and said that the instrumental cause of justification, the means or the tool that the church uses to bring a person into a state of justified grace, is the sacrament of baptism. The Reformers responded: "No, the sole instrumental cause is faith, not the sacrament. It is the faith that is in the heart of the believer. That's the instrument by which we are linked to the work of Christ for our salvation." The question of the instrumental cause of justification was no small issue at the time.

We call the Roman Catholic view of justification an analytical view. An analytical statement is one that is inherently true. It is a formal truth, a tautology. "Two plus two equals four." That statement is analytically true. That is, under analysis you examine what two and two are, and you say that it is the same thing that you find on the other side of the equation, which is four. It's a formal truth. It's not something that has to be confirmed by experimentation or observation. It's a mathematical truth. Another example of an analytical statement is "A bachelor is an unmarried man." Now, you've learned nothing in the predicate that wasn't already in the subject. You've said nothing new that defines the term *bachelor* than that which the word itself contains inherently. Now, both Protestants and Roman Catholics agree that in the final analysis, no one is justified until or unless God declares that person just. That declaration of God is a legal declaration by His own judgment. When we say that the Roman view is analytical, that means that God will not declare a person legally just unless or until that person, under analysis, is actually just. God doesn't count people just who aren't really just. That's why Rome in the sixteenth century stated that before God will ever declare someone justified, justice or righteousness must inhere within the soul of the person. No one really becomes justified until, under analysis, God reads his life, reads his soul, and sees nothing but righteousness there. If a person dies in mortal sin, he goes to hell. If a person dies with any sin, with any imperfection or blemish on his soul, that person cannot be admitted into heaven but must first go through the purging fires of purgatory, where those impurities are cleansed away until such time as righteousness is truly inherent in the believer.

You see what's at stake here. If I thought that to get into heaven I would have to arrive in a state of pure righteousness without any imperfections, no matter how much grace the church had for me, I would despair of ever having salvation. That is not good news. That is horrible news. We see why this is a significant theological issue. What must I do to be saved? The Reformation was about affirming the biblical gospel—the moment a person possesses saving faith, he is transferred from the kingdom of darkness into the kingdom of light, is declared to be just on the basis of the righteousness of Christ, and is adopted into the family of God. There is no purgatory, no ongoing need for confession and absolution and restoration of saving grace.

9

The Protestant
View of Justification

In the previous two chapters, we examined the Roman Catholic doctrine of justification. We now turn to the Reformation view of justification. The motto of the Reformation during the sixteenth century with respect to the doctrine of justification was *sola fide*. Added to that statement, the Reformers came up with four other *solas*: *sola Scriptura*, *sola gratia*, *solus Christus*, and *soli Deo gloria*. All five point to the central importance of the doctrine of justification by faith alone.

Sola fide simply means "by faith alone." We recall that the Roman communion also affirms that faith is necessary for justification. For Rome, it is a necessary condition but not a sufficient condition; you can't have justification without faith, but you can have faith without justification. So the controversy between Martin Luther and the other magisterial Reformers and Rome focused on this word *sola*, that justification is by faith alone. Now, mottoes can sometimes oversimplify matters. People might ask, Isn't it also necessary to repent in order to be justified? Yes, of course. But in the Reformation concept of faith, repentance is already understood to be an integral part of the faith that justifies. The term *sola fide* is simply shorthand for the idea that justification is by Christ alone, that we put our faith in what Jesus has done for us, and that by putting our faith in Him, we find our justification.

We can set forth the different formulae from the sixteenth century. The Roman Catholic view would be something like this: faith plus works equals justification. (Antinomianism, which abounds even in American evangelicalism, believes that faith equals justification minus works.) The Reformed, biblical view is that faith equals justification plus works. Now, notice on what side of the equation *works* appears. Any work that we do as Christians adds absolutely nothing to the ground of our justification. God does not declare us just because of any works that we do. It is by faith and faith alone that we receive the gift of justification. Paul writes: "Now we know that whatever the law says it speaks to those who are under the law, so that every mouth may be stopped, and the whole world may be held accountable to God. For by works of the law no human being will be justified in his sight, since through the law comes knowledge of sin" (Rom. 3:19–20).

Roman Catholic View of Justification
Faith + Works = Justification

Antinomian View of Justification
Faith = Justification – Works

Reformed View of Justification
Faith = Justification + Works

Paul then more fully explains the doctrine of justification by contrasting it to the works of the law:

> But now the righteousness of God has been manifested apart from the law, although the Law and the Prophets bear witness to it—the righteousness of God through faith in Jesus Christ for all who believe. For there is no distinction: for all have sinned and fall short of the glory of God, and are justified by his grace as a gift, through the redemption that is in Christ Jesus, whom God put forward as a propitiation by his blood, to be received by faith. This was to show God's righteousness, because in his divine forbearance he had passed over former sins. It was to show his righteousness at the present time, so that he might be just and the justifier of the one who has faith in Jesus. (Rom. 3:21–26)

In chapter 3, we noted Martin Luther's tower experience, a crisis that occurred when he was preparing his lectures on Paul's letter to the Romans. Luther came to an awakening that the righteousness by which we are justified, the righteousness of God, is not that righteousness by which God Himself is righteous but that righteousness that He provides for sinful people who receive it by faith. Now, at the heart of the controversy in the sixteenth century was the question, What is the ground by which God would ever declare someone righteous in His sight? Paul essentially raises the question asked in Psalm 130:3: "If you, O LORD, should mark iniquities, O Lord, who could stand?" That is, if we had to stand before God based on His perfect justice and perfect judgment of our performance, none of us would be able to stand. We would fall, because as Paul says, all have fallen short of the glory of God (Rom. 3:23). So this is the pressing question of justification: How can an unjust person ever be justified in the presence of a righteous and holy God?

In chapter 8, we identified the Roman Catholic view as analytical justification. An analytical statement is true by definition: "Two plus two is four" or "A bachelor is an unmarried man." There is nothing in the predicate that is not already contained in the subject. No new information is provided or added to the analysis of the subject itself. In the Roman view of justification, God will declare a person just only when, under His perfect analysis, He finds that the person is just, that righteousness is inherent in the person. Remember, people can't have that righteousness without faith. They can't have it without grace. They can't have it without the assistance of Christ. Nevertheless, given all those ingredients, in the final analysis, true righteousness must be present in the soul of a person before God will ever declare him just.

The Reformation view is that justification is synthetic rather than analytical. In a synthetic statement, something new is added in the predicate that is not analytically contained in the subject. If I said to you, "The bachelor was a poor man," I would have told you something new in the second part of the sentence that wasn't already contained simply in the word *bachelor*, because although all bachelors are unmarried men, not all bachelors are poor unmarried men. We have wealthy bachelors who are unmarried. And so when we talk about poverty or wealth, it's not something that's automatically inherent in the idea of bachelorhood. We are saying something new. There is a synthesis, as it were, something that was added to the subject.

The Reformation view of justification is that when God declares a person to be just in His sight, it's not because of what He finds in that person under His analysis, but rather it is on the grounds of something that is added to that person. And what is added to that person is the righteousness of Christ. Luther insisted that the righteousness by which we are justified is *extra nos*, apart from us or outside us. He also called it a *justicium alienum*—that is, an alien righteousness. It is not a righteousness that properly belongs to us but a righteousness that is foreign to us. It comes from outside the sphere of our own behavior. With both these terms, Luther was speaking about the righteousness of Christ.

Now, if any word was at the center of the firestorm of the sixteenth-century controversy and remains central to the debate even in our day, it is the word *imputation*. We really can't understand what the Reformation was about without understanding the central importance of this one word. Many meetings were held after the Diet of Worms to try to repair the schism that was taking place. Theologians from the Roman persuasion met with the magisterial Reformed theologians, trying to resolve the difficulties and to preserve the unity of the church, but the one word that they couldn't get past was *imputation*. What was the pressing issue?

In Romans 4, when Paul explains the doctrine of justification, he refers back to the patriarch Abraham in Genesis 15: "Abraham believed God, and it was counted to him as righteousness" (Rom. 4:3). Abraham was still a sinner. Throughout the narrative of the life and the actions of Abraham, Scripture reveals that he still had sin. Nevertheless, God considered him righteous because he believed in the promise. In this sense, to *impute* means "to transfer legally to somebody's account." So Paul speaks of God's counting Abraham as righteous, or reckoning him as righteous, even though in and of himself, Abraham was not yet righteous. This is vastly different from the Roman Catholic understanding of the infusion of grace, wherein, according to Rome, the grace of God is poured into the soul of the believer in the sacraments, and on the basis of that infused righteousness, that person becomes inherently righteous and is therefore judged by God to be righteous.

But Luther and the rest of the Reformers believed that the ground of our justification is God's imputing somebody else's righteousness to our account. And of course, what is reckoned to our account is the righteousness of Christ. The famous formula Luther used is *simul justus et peccator*. With this formula, Luther expressed that we are at one and the same time righteous or just and sinners. In one sense, we are just. In another sense, from a different perspective, we are sinners. In and of ourselves, under the analysis of God's scrutiny, we still have sin. We are still sinners. But by imputation and by faith in Jesus Christ, whose righteousness is now transferred to our account, we are considered just or righteous.

This is the very heart of the gospel. Will I be judged by my righteousness or by the righteousness of Christ? If I had to trust in my righteousness to get into heaven, I would despair of any possibility of ever being redeemed. But when we see that the righteousness that is ours by faith is the perfect righteousness of Christ, then we see how glorious the good news of the gospel is. The good news is simply this: I can be reconciled to God. I can be justified by God not on the basis of what I do but on the basis of what's been accomplished for me by Christ.

It's strange that the Roman church reacted so negatively to the idea of imputation, because in its own doctrine of the atonement, it teaches that our sins are imputed to Jesus on the cross; otherwise, there's no value of Jesus' atoning death for us. So the idea of atonement is there in Roman Catholic theology. Not only is it there, but when you talk about obtaining indulgences through the transfer of merit from the treasury of merit, how else do you receive those merits except by imputation? But at the heart of the gospel is a double imputation. My sin is imputed to Jesus. His righteousness is imputed to me. And in this twofold transaction we see that God, who does not negotiate sin, who doesn't compromise His own integrity with our salvation, but rather punishes sin fully and really after it has been imputed to Jesus, retains His own righteousness. He is both just and the justifier (Rom. 3:26).

My sin goes to Jesus. His righteousness comes to me in the sight of God. And this is worth dying for. This is worth dividing the church over. This is the article on which the church stands or falls because it's the article on which I stand or fall and the article on which you stand or fall.

10

Rome's Objections Answered

The Roman Catholic Church had some critical responses to the assertions and affirmations of the Protestant Reformation, including the excommunication of Martin Luther and his condemnation as a heretic by Pope Leo X. But three major issues came to the fore in the sixteenth century. First, what Rome heard coming from Luther and the Reformers was a type of antinomianism. *Antinomianism* is a theological word for a spirit of lawlessness or libertinism. Antinomians would say that all I have to do is believe, and I can live any kind of ungodly life that I choose and still be saved. We might call it cheap grace or easy-believ-ism. To counteract that, the Reformers had to make fine distinctions about what they meant by saving faith. As we saw in the previous chapter, Luther's for-mula was that we are justified by faith alone, but not by a faith that is alone. We'll look at that more deeply fur-ther on. The Reformers defined three specific elements of saving faith: *notitia*, *assensus*, and *fiducia*.

Notitia is the data. Nobody is justified by believing just anything. Our culture tells us that it doesn't mat-ter what you believe as long as you're sincere. If that were true, then you could put your trust in Satan, and if your trust in Satan were sincere, then you would be saved. That's absurd. Obviously, from a Christian and biblical perspective, it matters profoundly what you believe. The gospel has a content that one must under-stand with the mind and be informed about, and this includes the person and work of Jesus, His saving activ-ity. When we say that we're justified by faith, it's not by an empty faith or any faith in general. It is a faith in the person and work of Jesus.

Not only that, but the information or data that

we believe requires *assensus* or intellectual assent. We might tell someone that Jesus was born of a virgin, that He died a death that was an atoning death, and that He was raised for our justification, and then we ask that person, "Do you understand that?" The individual says, "Yes." We then ask, "Do you believe that?" At that point, we are asking whether the person affirms that those statements about Jesus are true and intellectually assents to the truth quotient of those propositions. But note that the Bible states that even the demons believe and tremble. Scripture means that the devil knows the facts, the data, and that not only does he know the data, he knows that the data is true. He tries everything to persuade people that it isn't true, but he knows better intellectually; at least cognitively, the devil knows the truth.

And so the third element of saving faith that the Reformers emphasized was *fiducia*, which is a personal trust in and volitional assent to Jesus. *Fiducia* is not simply an intellectual assent of the mind to the truth of the propositions, but it is the response of the heart in putting one's trust in the living Christ. The twentieth-century

Christian philosopher Gordon Clark challenged this, saying that even *fiducia* really is an intellectual exercise, that our mind is engaged in the act of trusting. I have no quarrel with that; I think he is absolutely right. Jonathan Edwards said something similar in the eighteenth century in his definitive work *Freedom of the Will*. Edwards defined the will as the mind choosing. Now, we distinguish between the mind and the will, between thinking and choosing, but Edwards said that you can't choose something that the mind rejects. When the mind has a certain affinity toward a proposition and embraces it, that's called choosing or willing. But there's no organ next to your liver or your spleen that is called the organ of the will. The will is an activity of the mind.

There is a difference between the assent that Satan has and the assent that we must have to be saved. We must agree to the sweetness of Christ, to the loveliness of Christ, to the excellency of Christ. Satan knows the truth of the person of Jesus objectively, but he hates the truth. He doesn't see or acknowledge the excellency of Jesus or the loveliness of Jesus because of his hatred, and that's what the Reformers perceived.

They also perceived that saving faith is not some easy affirmation. No, saving faith is produced by the regenerating work of God the Holy Spirit. And if it is real, if it is genuine, then we are linked by the sole instrument of justification by that faith to Christ and receive all that He is and all that He has done.

The second major objection of the Roman Catholic Church to the Reformation view of justification involved what Rome called a "legal fiction" concerning God. A fiction is something that is made up. It doesn't necessarily correspond with reality. Rome questioned how God, in His perfect righteousness and holiness, could ever declare a sinner to be just who in fact is not just. Doing so would involve God in a fictional declaration. The Reformers' response was somewhat simple. God declares a person just because God really imputes the real righteousness of Christ to that person. There's nothing fictional about Christ's righteousness, and there's nothing fictional about God's gracious imputation of that righteousness to those who, under analysis, do not have it themselves.

The third and biggest objection that Rome had in the sixteenth century concerned her understanding of James' teaching on justification. James wrote, "Was not Abraham our father justified by works when he offered up his son Isaac on the altar? . . . And the Scripture was fulfilled that says, 'Abraham believed God, and it was counted to him as righteousness'—and he was called a friend of God. You see that a person is justified by works and not by faith alone" (James 2:21–24). This text was brought up to Luther again and again, and in a weak moment, he even questioned the canonicity of the book of James, saying that James was an "epistle of straw." That was his retreat of the last resort.

When scholars look at the differences between Paul's teaching in Romans 3, 4, and 5 and James' teaching in James 2, they approach the discrepancies in different ways. Some say that the book of James was written before the epistle to the Romans, and that one of the things on Paul's agenda in writing Romans was to correct James' mistake. Others say that, no, Romans was written first and then James, and that part of James' agenda was to correct Paul's erroneous teaching.

Others say that it doesn't matter who wrote first or second; this is a clear example of the different Apostles of the first century having different theologies, and there's no consistent monolithic view of justification in the New Testament.

But those who believe that the Bible is the Word of God, and that both the book of James and the book of Romans are inspired by the Holy Spirit, must face the difficult task of reconciling the two books. Now, it would be nice to say that when James speaks of justification, he uses one Greek word, and that when Paul speaks of justification, he uses a different Greek word. But no, they both use the same Greek word, *dikaiosyne*. It would also be nice to say that James gave one patriarch as an example to explain his viewpoint and that Paul gave a different witness from history, but both refer to Abraham.

To reconcile the two epistles, we have to look at two important things. Though both biblical writers refer to Abraham, Paul uses Genesis 15, whereas James refers to Genesis 22. In Romans, Paul labors the point that Abraham was counted righteous before he had done any of the works of the law, before he had sacrificed Isaac on the altar. So from chapter 15 onward, Abraham was in a state of justification. But James refers to Genesis 22, which records Abraham's obedience to God's call to sacrifice his son Isaac on the altar. So when James is talking about Abraham's justification, he is referring primarily to the action that takes place in Genesis 22, whereas Paul is laboring the point that Abraham is justified freely and by grace, without having done any work, without ever deserving anything, in Genesis 15.

But the real key to understanding the differences in the writings of Paul and James is considering this: What question is Paul answering in Romans, and is it the same question that James is addressing in James 2? James asks: "What good is it, my brothers, if someone says he has faith but does not have works? Can that faith save him?" (James 2:14). He goes on: "If a brother or sister is poorly clothed and lacking in daily food, and one of you says to them, 'Go in peace, be warmed and filled,' without giving them the things needed for the body, what good is that? So also faith by itself, if it does not have works, is dead" (vv. 15–17).

James is asking, If somebody says that he has faith, but no works ensue from his profession of faith, can that kind of faith save him? How would Luther answer that question? He would say, "Of course not." That's why Luther said that we are justified by faith alone, but not by a faith that is alone. If the faith that we profess is a naked faith without any evidence of works, that is not saving faith. That's dead faith. The only kind of faith that justifies anybody is what Luther called a *fides viva*, a vital faith, a living faith that shows its life by obedience, by the works that follow from it.

Now, the ground of our justification is not found in the works that follow from our justification. But if the works don't follow from our justification, then that is proof that we're not justified people, that we don't have saving faith. James asks, If a person says that he has faith and has no works, will that faith save him? And he answers, No, that faith is dead, and it doesn't profit. He said: "But someone will say, 'You have faith and I have works.' Show me your faith apart from your works, and I will show you my faith by my works" (James 2:18). James' main consideration is the manifestation or the showing of faith. To whom? Does God have to wait to see my works to know whether my profession of faith is genuine? Did God not know that Abraham possessed saving faith all the way back in Genesis 15? Paul labored the point that once real, genuine faith was present, God counted Abraham righteous. But if I say to you, "I have faith and I have no works," what other way do I have to demonstrate to you that my profession of faith is authentic except by my obedience, by my manifestation of works?

Now, when Paul uses the term *justify*, he uses it in the highest theological sense of how a person is made just before God and is reconciled into a state of salvation. When James is speaking about justification here, he's talking about justifying a claim to faith before men. Jesus Himself used the term *justification* in a like manner, when he said, "Yet wisdom is justified by all her children" (Luke 7:35). What did He mean by that? He didn't mean that wisdom is brought into a reconciling relationship to God by having babies. He meant that an act that we think is wise will be demonstrated to be wise by the fruit it bears. So what James is addressing in his epistle is the demonstration or manifestation of true faith. When he says that Abraham our father was justified by works when he offered his son Isaac, James does not mean that Abraham was justified before God, but rather that he demonstrated that his claim to faith was genuine for all of us to see. James says that faith was working together with Abraham's works, and that by works his faith was made complete (James 2:22). And "the Scripture was fulfilled that says, 'Abraham believed God, and it was counted to him as righteousness'" (v. 23). Abraham was justified not in the sight of God but in the sight of men. His profession of faith was vindicated. His soul was put in a state of reconciliation.

But Paul addresses the doctrine of justification in the sense of our ultimate reconciliation with a just and holy God. He writes the epistle to the Romans to explain how ultimate salvation is accomplished. He labors the point that we are justified not by the works of the law but by faith, apart from the works of the law. We are justified not by our own righteousness but by the righteousness of Christ.

We end by affirming that the doctrine of justification by faith alone is really not hard to understand. We do not need a Ph.D. in theology to plumb the contents of the doctrine. But as simple as it is, it can be one of the hardest truths of Scripture to fully grasp. We can do nothing to earn, to deserve, or to add to the merit of Jesus Christ. When we stand before the judgment seat of God, we come with nothing in our hand except the righteousness of Christ. We cling to the cross of Christ and put our trust in Him and in Him alone. That's why the Reformers always ended their confession with the words *soli Deo gloria*, "to God alone be the glory," because salvation is of the Lord.

About the Author

Dr. R.C. Sproul was founder of Ligonier Ministries, founding pastor of Saint Andrew's Chapel in Sanford, Fla., first president of Reformation Bible College, and executive editor of *Tabletalk* magazine. His radio program, *Renewing Your Mind*, is still broadcast daily on hundreds of radio stations around the world and can also be heard online. He was author of more than one hundred books, including *The Holiness of God*, *Chosen by God*, and *Everyone's a Theologian*. He was recognized throughout the world for his articulate defense of the inerrancy of Scripture and the need for God's people to stand with conviction upon His Word.